DOG WATCHING

Brucer, 1992

DOG WATCHING

Robin Schwartz

Takarajima Books

To Noah and Jonah, and to the strays

Dog Watching

Copyright © 1995 by Takarajima Books, Inc.

Photographs and preface copyright © 1995 by Robin Schwartz

All rights reserved under International and Pan-American Copyright Conventions.

No part of this book may be reproduced in any manner without the prior written permission from the publisher and the copyright holder.

Takarajima Books, 200 Varick Street, New York, NY 10014
Tel: (212) 675-1944, Fax: (212) 255-5731

Book and cover design: Germaine Clair
Endsheet pattern based on a design by Huichol artist Luis Ruiz

The staff at Takarajima Books for *Dog Watching* is:
Akihiko Miyanaga, Publisher
Kiyotaka Yaguchi, Assistant publisher

ISBN: 1-883489-14-8

Library of Congress Card Number: 94-061940

Printed and bound by C & C Offset Printing Co., Ltd., Hong Kong

PREFACE

Animals are the passion and obsession that fuel my imagination. The boundary line separating people and animals has always been blurred for me, and perhaps because of that, I try to develop a dialogue with my subjects, whatever their species. My goal while photographing is to show each animal as a unique individual. Eye contact is an important factor in the portraits, representing my subjects' conscious response to me and our encounter. Photography records these memories.

My relationship to "picturing animals" dates all the way back to childhood, when I brought home stray wanderers and believed the animal illustrations I saw in books came to life. At age ten, I began photographing my cat-brother Whitey, dressed in doll clothes. Later, in graduate school in Brooklyn, I found comfort and a spiritual connection in photographing the stray dogs that roamed the streets of New York and New Jersey. On my own and feeling lost, I often had the uncanny feeling, when I looked into the eyes of these abandoned creatures, that I was seeing myself. Since that time, I have continued to photograph animals, concentrating on dogs and primates in various urban and rural setting and inside private homes. I believe that animals such as dogs, kept most often as pets, offer us a unique glimpse into the heart of the human culture that surrounds them. The relationship of dog and owner cuts across class-structure, and reveals a lot about the culture's models of kinship, and of myth. On a less exalted level, I simply love dogs. I have found great humanity, love, respect, adventure and comfort in their company. As I hope *Dog Watching* shows.

Robin Schwartz

ACKNOWLEDGEMENTS

I am grateful to Takarajima Books and Akihiko Miyanaga for publishing a book of my dog photographs. Their encouragement gave me the incentive to photograph dogs from a new perspective, a project which evolved into the *Dog Watching* book. I especially wish to thank Kiyotaka Yaguchi for his suggestions and for bringing my photographs into his home. I cannot imagine this book without Germaine Clair. She not only designed *Dog Watching,* but also sifted through hundreds of prints, endlessly editing and resequencing the photos. I thank Barbara Head Millstein and Merry Foresta, whose faith in my photography has encouraged and sustained me through many doubtful times. I thank my husband, Robert Forman, for his companionship during many days that turned into dog photo sessions. And I thank my tolerant whippet, Jonah, who sat on the laps of three different Santa Clause' in 1993, while I scouted out the other dogs waiting on line to have their pictures taken with Santa. Most of all, I wish to thank the many people who patiently permitted me to photograph their dogs.

Raggs, 1987

Momma, 1993

Piazzi and Lucy, 1988

Martin and Guinivere, 1987

Mural, 1981

Rosie with Dutchie, Fritzie, Beanie and Trixie, 1993

Sport, Commissioner Gordon, Flurry, Abbey and Bullet, 1994

Molly, 1993

Mac, 1993

Rocky and Ashley, 1987

Rocky and Ashley, 1987

The Whisper, 1987

The Ride, 1987

Discipline, "stay" 1987

Jake and Tabitha, 1990

Missy and Pee Dee Rose Angelina, 1987

Hot Dog at Tepic Fair, 1992

Pete, Hoboken K-9, 1993

Punkie, 1994

Flurry, Mischi, Quiche, Bogey, Bullet, and Sport, 1994

Redhook Man and his Dog, 1983

Jonah, 1992

Cheval, 1993

Central Park Swimmer, 1993

Bozo and Jackie, 1987

Sophie, 1994

Chained Dog Under Car, 1984

Poodle, 1982

Jake and Mugs, 1990

Max and Lilypod, 1981

Kojak, Clancy, Jackie, Heart and Ferguson, 1988

Buster, 1988

Governor of Tepic's Xoloitzcuinti, (Mexican Hairless Dog), 1992

Hoboken Lady and her Dogs, 1983

Dorje and Vajra, 1993

E-me Lou and Zeb, 1990

Punkie and Crystal, 1994

Spike, 1987

Pansy, 1993

Cocaine, 1987

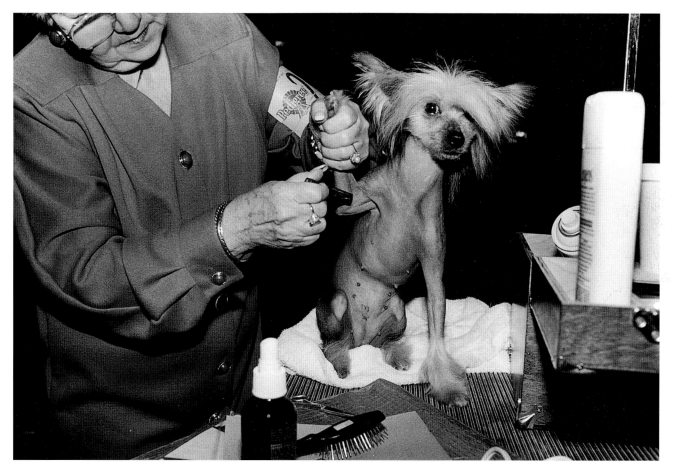

Chinese Crested, Westminister Kennel Club, 1993

Filene and Quincy, POWERS Benefit Fashion Show, 1993

Muggsie, 1993

Commissioner Gordon, 1994

Sophia, 1993

Amy Bo Bo, 1994

Sophie, 1994

Charlie, 1993

Bugsy, 1993

Tarzan's Dog, 1988

Elizabeth and Rockie, 1994

Williamsburg Barbershop, 1980

Jonah, 1993

Hoboken Girl Taking Stray Home, 1985

Blue and Brutus, 1993

Maximilian, Priscilla and Pandora, 1993

Chrissy, Cakes and Alec, 1993

Nick, Nora and Asta, 1993

Governor of Tepic's Xoloitzcuintles (Mexican Hairless Dogs), 1992

Springfield Dogs, 1980

Parkslope Dog, 1983

Logan, Charlie, Morgan, Paris and Robbie with Santa Claus, 1993

Momma, 1993

Genghis, 1985

Mischi and Bogey, 1994

Jonah, 1993

Couple on a Mattress, 1984

Susie, 1984

Bozo, 1987

Pee Dee Rose Angelina, 1987

Pee Dee in the Car, 1987

Pee Dee Catching Bone Biscuit, 1987

Pee Dee Drinking, 1987

Tired Pee Dee, 1987

Deputy, Fox and Blitz, 1994

Roadside Stray, 1984

Bozo, 1987

Pit Bull Pups, 1993

George and Frog, 1993

Vana and Miracle, 1990

Squeaky and Happy, 1989

Natasha and Rocky, 1993

Dorje and Shoshe, 1993

Tillie and Ziggy, 1994

Puck and Oberon, 1993

Blaze, 1993

Central Park Wader, 1993

Bull Terrier and Pit Bull Pups, 1985

Chrissy and Priority, 1993

Maggie and Ebony, 1993

Spanky and Jane, 1994

Oberon and Puck, 1994

Fidget, 1994

Squeaky and Happy, 1989

Crystal and her Three Week Old Pup, 1994

Strays on Car, 1987

Quiche, Abbey, Flurry, Wilma, Commissioner Gordon, Bullet, Sport and Buzz, 1994

Eliza Doolittle, Zoe, Schultz a.k.a. Henry Higgens, 1994

Pee Dee Sleeping, 1987